# HEALTH CARE

## It Can be Fixed!

*"The truth about Health Care"*

## Fritz Scheffel

Eloquent Books

New York, New York

**HEALTH CARE – It Can be Fixed**

Copyright 2007 - All rights reserved - Fritz Scheffel

Eloquent Books
*An imprint of Writers Literary & Publishing Services, Inc.*
845 Third Avenue, 6th Floor - 6016
New York, NY 10022
www.eloquentbooks.com

ISBN 978-0-9795935-7-4
Printed in the United States of America

Cover Design: Mark Bredt
Photo/Illustration by: Scott Weichert / www.dreamstime.com

## ACKNOWLEDGEMENTS

I have been blessed with a wonderful wife for over forty years. During this time Judy and I have endured the usual ups and downs of life. We have also shared a journey of faith and hope as well as a growing "love affair". Without her love and encouragement this book could not have happened and I take this opportunity to say "THANK YOU".

I am also thankful to Katherine Parson and Barbara Gieseking for their friendship, enthusiastic encouragement and editing help. Their contributions made this a better book.

# TABLE OF CONTENTS

# INTRODUCTION

Americans are uneasy about the cost and availability of health care in the U.S. I hope this book will begin the process of change in this country through an understanding of what health care was before government involvement, how we got in this mess and what we can do about it. The system is broken as a result of political greed, plain and simple. With the economic power of this country there is no reason we cannot have the very best and affordable health care system in the world. My fear is that if we do not begin the process of making it right, it may never happen. Roughly speaking, Americans up to age 50 have grown up "expecting" a system to work because our politicians have teased us over and over that they can provide the cure. NOTHING could be further from the truth.

In this book we will examine all parts of what I think make up "health care". The various parts include government, insurance companies, drug manufacturers, pharmacy, hospitals, and let's not forget lawyers. My dictionary does not even have the word "health care" in it, so it is important to understand what we mean when we talk about health care or health care. In this book we look at the total picture of our health needs and define what health care really is.

When I began to think about doing this book, I stopped at one of the large book stores and looked through shelves and shelves of books on health. Everything from diets, to exercise, allergies, vitamins, holistic remedies, and herbs had book after book written about the wonders of this and that. I could not find one single book that will encompass what you will find in this book. I then wondered why there was no publication that addressed the reasons we have a crisis that concerns everyone. There are a lot of "moving parts" to health care and the subject needs to be presented in a non-biased way to be credible. The more I thought about it, the more I realized I have nothing to sell, except this book. I have experience in all facets of what I call health care. Since I am no longer associated in any way with the health care industry, I can be objective and identify the culprits who have caused this mess.

This book will not have a lot of statistics, nor will it have any advice on the best diets, or recommendations on current health insurance plans. Instead you will find examples of my real life experiences that I hope will help you better understand what health care really is. With a better understanding, I am confident you will come to a solid realization that we all need to be involved in changing this mess. We cannot afford to rely on others to make decisions about our health care for us. I did very limited research for this book I am not creative enough to make this "stuff" up and as a result everything in this book is true. My opinions and suggestions for change are reasoned and thoughtful suggestions that have no other purpose other than to help make things better for everyone. I vividly express my opinions to make points I think are extremely important and I am not afraid to name those responsible for this disaster we have too long called "health care".

I am anxious to do my part to show we all can take charge of our individual lives. As I was conceptually putting this book together in my head and on paper I became so enthused that I committed myself to better health. I committed to losing 110 pounds and while writing this book lost a total of 40 pounds and counting. I would not have any credibility with you if I could not do for myself that which I propose others do. Besides, I want to a least look good when we meet.

By the end of the book, I will have offered what I think is a blueprint for how health care can work. It is my sincere hope that when you have finished the book you will accept that your health is something you can take charge of, and mad enough at those responsible for this mess to enlist others to help you make a difference. It starts with you and me. Have a great, blessed and healthy life.

Fritz Scheffel
American

## GOVERNMENT'S ROLE

Let's get started by looking at how health care looked before the government and insurance companies became involved. Things like health care were very simple back then. When people got sick they went to their family doctor to determine their illness and receive treatment. After the visit, they paid the doctor for services rendered and if prescriptions were issued they were taken to their pharmacy to be filled. There was no such thing as an "insurance plan" that covered health care needs such as doctor visits, hospital visits, or prescriptions. As a result, you paid for what you needed. No health insurance also meant that if a new baby was born in the hospital, the new parents paid the hospital for their stay and services, and also paid the doctor for the delivery.

There may have been some indemnity plans that looked like health insurance available for those that could afford it. Some of these indemnity plans are still available today and one such company is best known for using a duck in their advertising. An indemnity plan is a type of insurance where you pick the illness you think may affect you and pay premiums. Usually these plans will have a fixed amount stated in the policy that it will pay toward treatment for that illness.

In those days doctors were usually called "GP's" or general practitioners. They were on call twenty-four hours a day with the local hospital serving as the call center. Each morning their first stop was usually the hospital to check on their patients before arriving at their office. If necessary, these doctors were also surgeons and generally took care of all their patient's medical needs. It was easy to get to know your doctor personally because in most cases they had been the family's doctor for many years. In those days everyone relied on "their" doctor to make the decision to call in a specialist if the illness or surgery required advanced skills and education.

We might ask here, "Where have the family doctors gone?" because as I see it they have become extinct. Stay tuned and I will tell you why.

In those earlier times, without insurance plans, all doctors had huge accounts receivable. They treated all of their patients even though they knew they would probably never get paid. No doctor wanted to have the reputation of turning away a sick child just because the parents could not pay, so they treated any who desperately needed care. Remember, this was before credit cards came into existence, so you either had the money or you asked the doctor to "send a bill" which meant accounts receivable. Look, back then, before government programs, if you were not sick, you did not go to the doctor, that's just the way it was. Instead they would go to their local pharmacy to purchase something for whatever symptoms they were afflicted with. As a pharmacist, there were many times I strongly recommended someone go to the hospital immediately and call their doctor because I felt they were really sick and did not know it.

The following situation happened a lot. Very few people made the effort to get annual physical exams on their own. When the local "life" insurance salesman called they would buy an insurance policy because insurance companies, wanting to be sure one was healthy enough to qualify for additional insurance, *required* a physical exam. Since the insurance company paid for the exam people could "afford" to go to the doctor for a physical.

As an introduction to "government health care" I would like to state here that ***I can think of no government program that has worked for the good of our citizens.*** I am not speaking just of health care programs, but **ANY** government program. The politicians we have elected to office have learned that words are enough to convince American voters that they have good intentions. Even now as I am writing this book the campaigns are kicking off for offices to be voted on in the year 2008 and some of the aspirants are claiming "they will fix health care" as part of their platform. NOTE: This is a family book and I cannot tell you exactly what I think of these promises, but it is not very good.

Here are some examples of failed government programs. These examples should serve as warnings to us about political promises. The first example of failure is a look at Medicare and Medicaid programs initiated in the

1960's. Not only are they super expensive for the government to keep funding, but there are eligibility limits, coverage limits and other rules and regulations that need to be followed. If this is the only health care coverage available to you, be prepared to give up your freedoms and dignity because the government now owns you.

Not only are government health care programs an example of failed political promises, look at government run education programs. Every politician I listen to "promises" to fix education by spending more money "on education". We need to wake up and realize that just spending more money is not a solution that will fix a problem. Getting education and health care **OUT** of government control is the solution. We owe it to our children to educate them enough to at least balance a checkbook.

A political speech for any office in the United States that cites the Canadian Health Care System as an example of a workable "universal" health care system should be reason enough to disqualify the politician from holding any political office, EVER. During the recent elections in Canada to elect a new leader for the country, every politician promised to "fix" the Canadian system. Now, think about this, if a government system such as the Canadian Health Care System has been in existence for over thirty years and it still has massive problems, what do you think the odds are that it will be fixed next year?

How about this? Way too many of our citizens do not save money toward their retirement because they think Social Security is going to be there when they retire. Just another "hoax" our elected politicians talk about because they know their talk and good intentions will keep them in office. COME ON AMERICA!!!! THE POLITICIANS WE ELECT ARE "STEALING" OUR MONEY THROUGH TAXATION AND FEEDING US CRUMBS. To make things worse they keep telling us about all the good things they do for us. LET'S GET REAL!!! Politicians are only interested in POWER. They know if we must rely on them for everything, they OWN us and that equates to POWER over our lives.

I feel better now that I have vented, so let's get back on track. How did we get in this mess? To the best of my recollection, it started in the early 1960's when LBJ came up with a catchy name "The Great Society". They were going to create government programs to take care of the poor. They first created a program where "the poor" could get free prescriptions, then free doctor visits, then food stamps and I think you get the idea. Not everyone qualified for these 'benefits", but they really began to change the face of our nation from a society of free enterprise health care to a health care welfare state. People began to believe these government programs were "free" and there was no one to tell them any different, certainly not politicians. I have no way of measuring this but I think these "great society gifts" and the phrases they spoke like "helping the poor" initiated an era where elected politicians began staying in office for longer and longer periods of time. All a politician had to do to stay in office was give government handouts to his/her constituency and re-election was almost automatic.

Not only did this "Great Society" begin to change the way government worked, but it changed cultures as well.

At the time in South Texas where I lived and worked, many of my friends and neighbors were of Mexican descent. Mexican families had a tradition which went like this. Grandparents were taken care of by the grandchildren while parents worked to support the family. The grandchildren worked at odd jobs to earn money for the grandparents. If grandparents needed something like a trip to the doctor, the grandchild provided the means or transportation to the grocery store. Whatever the grandparents needed was usually provided by the grandchildren. This practice continued generation after generation.

Now along comes the government with their "free" programs that pay for the grandparent's doctor visit, hospital stay, and/or prescriptions and sometimes even the transportation. Well, guess what, the grandchildren soon realized they were not needed in the grand scheme of things and instead of having to give their earnings to the grandparents they could keep the money. Again guess what, they spent that money on themselves, probably buying alcohol and maybe illicit drugs and soon learned they need not work to support grandparents.

Obviously the politicians knew they could buy votes with these programs and the saddest part of all, the American people (voters) never realized or understood that their tax dollars were paying for the freebies. The modern day term for these programs is "entitlements" and they have become so large and so much a part of our culture that they will be hard to end. How hard? Try talking to a liberal sometime and at the same time make an argument for doing away with entitlements and you will see how hard it is going to be ending them. The only way, as I see it, is through educating the American voter about what these entitlement programs really represent and the dangers to the U.S. economy of continuing them. I DO NOT WANT MY CHILDREN AND GRANDCHILDREN TO BE SADDLED WITH THESE "MISTAKES". This is a big reason for this book!!

The creation of these programs became an opportunity for corporations like drug companies and insurance companies. Government agencies assigned to administer these entitlement programs were unable to keep up with the rapid growth, and citizens who for the most part did not have access to "free enterprise" health care facilities flooded doctor's offices. Insurance companies became involved in providing the administrative procedures and drug companies experienced an increase in the sale of prescription drugs. We will get more deeply into the Insurance and Drug Company sides of the issue later in the book, but needless to say, they were eager to be involved because they smelled money.

In the beginning the doctor's loved the program. Let's remember that a lot of their patients could not pay for the doctor's services and as a result the doctors carried large accounts receivable balances. Now with these new programs the doctor thinks "wow" here is the government paying me to treat these people I have previously been treating "for free".

At this time in the evolution of health care I owned a pharmacy in a relatively small town. There were two hospitals, about fifteen doctors and probably six pharmacies that made up the health care system. As a pharmacist I knew all of the doctors personally and as time went by I developed a sense of the doctor's "abilities" for lack of a better term. This was not hard to do because their prescribing habits told me a lot about them professionally. When I serviced their patients with prescriptions, I could see the results of their prescribing. I bring this up to make a point. Back then health care was simple, it started with the doctor, then the pharmacist and/or the hospital if necessary.

So let's look at what happened in this new evolving "free" program. The doctor was hooked because he was getting paid for his services, the patients are hooked on "free" health care, the drug companies probably did not object to what was happening because they sold more drugs. Pharmacy was forced to go along or be left out of this new 'free' phenomenon. Later in the book I will expand on pharmacy and the drug companies.

Let's advance the health care system forward and look at how things have changed. Now, the first concern a sick person has is "am I covered by insurance", then which doctor to go to. This seems like a simple question, but today practically all doctors have become specialists. Then, if you find the right doctor, and can fit into their schedule, the question is, do they accept insurance, and if drugs are needed, will they be covered and if not covered, can you afford them?

To me, the most grievous sin the government committed back then, and is still committing today, is that they "defined" health care for us. They made us believe that health care meant the same for everyone. The government wanted us to think if they provided the money, everyone could enjoy better health, and thus was born what is charitably called "socialized medicine". As a side note, about that time the government gave birth to "socialized retirement" and called it "social security". This is not the place to discuss the foibles of social security, but understand the similarities with socialized medicine.

So, what is health care? "Health care" has a different meaning for every individual. In no way can health care be thought of as a program that will make all of us healthier. For one person good health may mean losing weight. For another it may mean controlling allergies for a better quality of life. For another good health may mean treating and dealing with Parkinson's disease, or cancer, or heart problems, or any number of ailments that collectively are part of "life". When all of us really understand the true meaning of "health care" we can, and must effect change.

Going to a doctor and getting a prescription to alleviate the symptoms of an allergy will not cure the person, only relieve the symptoms and perhaps make their quality of life better. If an individual's health is threatened by being overweight, that person needs to make the decision to lose weight or suffer the consequences. If someone comes down with cancer or any number of other diseases, the doctors use medications or surgery to conquer the disease and treatments can be expensive and unfortunately not always successful. Tough love says this is life. Who knows what caused the disease, it could have been life style, maybe one's DNA or gene make up contributed, or maybe it was bad luck.

The point of all of this is that health care means something different to everyone and the government has gotten all of us off focus with their incessant pandering. We focus on thinking the government can throw money at something and the problem will go away. We all need a good dose of reality. The truth is that whatever health care plans we have, or expect, or desire, are nothing more than vehicles to pay for medical services. Having insurance is not going to make anyone healthier, nor will taking drugs make someone healthy. Going to a doctor or hospital may treat illnesses or diseases, but they can do nothing more to make one healthier.

The best corollary I can think of is your car. Just because you have insurance on your vehicle does not mean it will run any better. In fact your car will only continue to run if you maintain it properly and put the right fuels in it. Our bodies are no different, proper care is essential to good health. The government cannot enact legislation to give us good health, the government is only looking for more taxes and more control of each of us, and our good health is not part of their constitutional responsibilities. Ultimately our "good health" is our INDIVIDUAL responsibility.

Depending on the government **WILL NOT** make you richer, but it **WILL** make you poorer!

**Quote of the Day**: "*The best minds are not in government. If any were, business would hire them away.*" – **Ronald Reagan**

## INSURANCE COMPANIES

When I started in pharmacy in 1959, I do not recall insurance companies having a major role in the health care industry, but they were in the early stages of providing health plans. As pharmacists, our attitude was that it was the customer's responsibility to keep records of their prescription purchases. Shortly after politicians created the first government sponsored health care plan, insurance companies began to be a big part of health care. Pharmacists had to create ways of keeping better records, which led to the need for computers in pharmacy, but that's a whole different story.

As government health care programs expanded and adjusted, insurance companies became even more involved. They kept track of prescriptions and drugs, as well as pricing for the government. As all of these changes took place, I could see there was no future in pharmacy because insurance companies took away the profitability.

Look around today, there are no independent pharmacies left.

In the October 16, 2006 issue of USA TODAY the cover story was titled "Consumer unease with U.S. health care grows". The whole story was a report on a "survey" taken in September of 2006, and sponsored by USA TODAY, ABC News and the Kaiser Family Foundation. The Kaiser Family Foundation is an independent organization that studies major health care issues for the non-insured and probably provides information and data to anyone interested. Of course USA TODAY and ABC News were probably a part of the survey to get as much negative news as possible. Don't you get tired of seeing these human interest stories on TV when the media highlights a single tragedy with victims grieving their loss? Not only have they suffered pain or loss, but they must endure the inevitable question "what are you feeling now?"

I am not a fan of surveys because they are used to make news and can be slanted or biased toward a desired response. To quote from the paper, "The poll found a growing unease in America about the rising cost of health care, confusion about the causes and a desire for major reform." There are three points in this statement and two of them are reasons for this book, those being confusion about the cause, and a desire for major reform.

Let's take a look at some simple reasons costs are going up.

1) Drugs are more expensive (and we will examine why).

2) Hospital costs have risen because they must treat anyone who shows up in need regardless of their ability to pay or not. If you are wondering why a hospital would provide free service, well either our elected politicians passed a law or a government bureaucracy ruled hospitals must provide service. This practice is sometimes called "an unfunded mandate".

3) Law suits are brought on by lawyers, but only if some "victim" is willing to allow the law suit.

4) Doctors must charge more to pay for increased mal-practice insurance costs among other reasons. (see #3 above)

I hope you will not look at this list and think the examples are normal within the health care system. They may be normal in today's environment, but they do not have to be part of a successful health care system. We will examine these issues and more in this book and I hope you come away with the knowledge that government's intervention and/or lack of appropriate regulation affected health care in ways that will make your blood boil. Politicians have "blown so much smoke" at all of us that we have a hard time seeing the truth. They are only taking advantage of a constituency that will not ask questions when the "gifts" start coming. It is very sad that we have succumbed to the pandering politicians who promise something without telling us the cost. So, for the most part we, the American people, are largely to blame for letting ourselves get "snookered"

Forgive me for digressing. Insurance companies have a role in health care. For the most part I think insurance companies get too much blame for the crisis in health care, but they have assumed some roles that give them too much control over your health and mine. That is wrong. At the same time, I will say that I think insurance companies are blameless when it comes to excessive profits. They are a great example of "free enterprise" and I am a fan of free enterprise.

Health insurance, by definition, is supposed to be protection for you and me against catastrophic illnesses and accidents. In the same way, home owners insure their home against the unforeseen; fire, tornado, hurricanes, and other "acts of God" that are not normal every day happenings. As a home owner you expect to have your monthly mortgage payment and usual and customary maintenance expenses, home owner insurance premiums, repairs for appliances, furniture upgrades, repainting, carpet replacement and the list goes on. These expenses must be budgeted for by the owner and guess what, if the home owner cannot afford these expenses they probably are living in too much house. If there is an insurance claim the home owner pays a co-pay and the insurance company pays the rest of the original value, no more. As time goes on the home value appreciates, and the replacement costs of the contents also increases, and your insurance needs to be reviewed annually so adjustments can be made. Claims paid by insurance companies are never considered "profit" for the home owner. In other words insurance pays only to make the insured whole at an agreed upon value.

The same concept works for your car insurance and in each case the owner is allowed to make a decision to pay more in premiums to have a lower co-pay, or a lower premium for a higher co-pay. The concept is simple, right? Guess what, if you have a claim of any size after an accident your subsequent premiums will go up. As it turns out, the insurance companies are in business to make a profit, what a concept.

In order to control health care costs Americans must manage their health better. Far too many feel they can neglect their health because doctors and drugs can fix just about anything. The unfortunate thinking of far too many Americans is "if I have health insurance I will only have to pay co-pays". We need to alter this thinking for any meaningful changes to occur. If change is going to occur it cannot be mandated by the government because it would be more of the same. Change will have to begin with every American wanting to do their part to fix the system. It can be done! I want to emphasize again, this book is designed to show Americans how we got in this mess and how to fix the system. On paper the solution will be logical and seem simple, but the transitional period for any worthwhile change may be painful for some.

I was listening to talk radio the other day because the topic was "health care" and sure enough one of the callers was already complaining. He was receiving heath care insurance from his employer and was lamenting how much it would cost him out of his pocket if he had to provide his own insurance. This is so sad! I cannot repeat it enough, when we correct our health care system in this country, the whole economy will be robust and vibrant, providing opportunities for everyone to be successful and even more the envy of the world. Rising water lifts all ships!

## CURRENT HEALTH INSURANCE PLANS:

The following will list various health plans in existence today with a very brief description of plan features. For years I was licensed to sell these programs and I have a hard time keeping the different features clear in my mind. It is no wonder that confusion reigns and contributes to everyone making decisions about coverage, costs, and limitations that really may not be in their own best interest. This information is provided as examples of differences between programs and in no way intended as a recommendation of any health care plan.

Before discussing various health plans let us be sure we understand some basics about what health insurance does. Health insurance provides coverage for medicine, doctor visits, emergency room visits, hospital stays, and other medical expenses. Policies differ in what is covered, the size of the deductible and/or co-payments (often referred to as co-pays). Many people receive health insurance from their employer as a "benefit", while others must shop around for the right policy or one they can afford.

Here is a list of features that will be found in most of the insurance plans, if not all of them. By listing them and making them known to everyone it will become obvious why my proposed changes to the health care system will be beneficial to all.

- Health insurance policies are generally written for a twelve-month period of time. (In case you are wondering why there are term limits, it helps carriers identify losses more quickly and make changes before they lose too much money)

- Plans are written to provide the desired benefits for the group or individual. The more benefits that are included such as maternity, dental, and vision, the higher the premiums.

- Plans usually require deductible amounts. These out of pocket dollars must be spent by the individual(s) before insurance coverage kicks in and benefits are received.

- In addition to deductible amounts that need to be spent before insurance pays, individuals will usually be responsible for co-pays for each visit or service.

- If an employee leaves his/her job for any reason and they are covered by the business's group insurance plan, coverage ceases.

- There is a master health insurance computer located somewhere which keeps track of individual's health records If you have received medical treatments which were paid for by an insurance plan your records are stored. Trying to hide medical problems from an insurance company is virtually impossible.

- Pre-existing medical problems will probably not be covered by insurance plans. Smokers may not qualify for coverage, cancer survivors may not be covered in future plans and the list goes on.

- All insurance plans I have seen have policy reimbursement limits for either annual or life time dollars.

Let us now look at some existing insurance plans, how they work and the advantages and disadvantages of each.

## Health Maintenance Organization (HMO)

An HMO is a type of managed health care system. A group of doctors and other medical professionals offer care through the HMO for a ***flat monthly rate*** with no deductibles.

- Only visits to professionals ***within*** the HMO network are covered by the policy.
- All visits, prescriptions and other care must be ***cleared*** by the HMO in order to be covered.
- Your primary physician within the HMO will handle ***referrals***.

## Preferred Provider Organization (PPO)

A PPO is similar to an HMO, but ***care is paid for as it is received*** instead of in advance in the form of a scheduled fee. By scheduled fee we mean fees that members pay for services and these fees are set by the PPO.

- More flexibility by allowing for visits to out-of-network professionals at a greater expense to the policy holder.
- Visits within the network require only the payment of a small fee.
- There is often a deductible for out-of-network expenses and a higher co-payment.

- Your primary physician within the network will handle referrals to specialists that will be covered by the PPO.
- After any visit you must submit a claim and you will be reimbursed for the visit minus your co-payment.

## Health Savings Accounts (HAS)

A tax advantaged savings plan (a financial account with various restrictions) available to taxpayers in the United States to cover current and future medical expenses.

- It allows money to be put in ***before tax*** is paid on it.
- It allows you to withdraw the money ***tax free*** for qualified medical expenses.
- A person must be covered by a High Deductible Health Plan (HDHP) to be eligible for an HSA.
- The premium for a HDHP generally is less than the premium for traditional health care coverage.
- The amount you can save in this plan is determined by the policy (this is not a place to hide money tax free).
- A good option for self-employed individuals.

## Health Reimbursement Arrangements (HRA)

HRAs (also known as 105 plans) represent the newest development in employer-sponsored health benefits.

- Employers designate a fixed annual amount for employees to spend, **_tax-free_**, on their choice of sickness or wellness expenses.

- Unused amounts each year may be carried forward indefinitely.

- Unused amounts may be given to former employees tax-free to fund health costs during retirement.

Employers who provide health insurance policies for their employees have been raising annual deductibles and employee co-pays every year, both to save money and to give employees incentives to make wise health care choices. However, this forces employees to spend their own after-tax dollars for out-of-pocket expenses, needlessly wasting 25-50%, by throwing away the tax deduction for these amounts.

### Fee-For-Service (FFS)

FFS plans are also called indemnity plans and I have discussed them before in another chapter. These plans allow for visits to any medical professional. These plans are extremely flexible by allowing you to make most of the decisions about your personal care. In other words, if you think you could possibly come down with specific illnesses like cancer, diabetes, or heart problems, you have the freedom to buy coverage for these illnesses.

- After a visit you pay the bill and then submit a claim to the insurance company for reimbursement.

- The only limitations are that services provided must be specified in the policy in order for a claim to be accepted.

- These plans are not considered "managed" care plans, and the result is higher deductibles and co-payments.

## Medicare

Medicare is a federal program which provides health insurance for qualified individuals over the age of 65. Enrolled individuals must pay deductibles and co-payments, but many of their medical costs are covered by the program. Medicare is less comprehensive than the above programs, but it is an important source of post-retirement health care.

Medicare is divided into three parts. Part A covers hospital bills and home health care, Part B covers doctor bills and outpatient services such as "physical therapy", and Part C provides the option to choose from a package of health care plans. You should enroll as soon as you qualify because, at that time, you can receive coverage even if you have health problems. Later you may no longer qualify to automatically receive coverage because of health issues, so this free period is very important.

## Accident Insurance

Here is an example of a type of policy that would cover you only if you were injured in an accident. It covers the medical expenses as the result of a bodily injury or death. This does not cover self-inflicted injury, intentional harm from another person, homicide, sickness or death from natural causes.

## SUMMARY

As you can see there are many options out there in the market place. None of the plans are going to make you rich, but they may help you from losing everything due to severe illness or disease. The more I study the above plans the better I like my idea. There is a new proposal recently introduced by President Bush that I think is a step in the right direction, but has no chance of passage with Congress.

President Bush has proposed using the tax system to encourage change and bring about better and more affordable health care. He has proposed that if an employee is receiving health care benefits on the job and the value is more than $15,000 annually, the employee would pay taxes on the excess. Conversely, if an individual is purchasing health insurance out of his pocket, that he receive tax credits up to the $15,000. I think his plan would also allow associations to which a person may belong to set up group plans. This proposal is getting closer to "free enterprise health care" and letting the market determine costs. I think this proposal by our president has no chance of coming into being because the politicians would lose some tax revenue and if enacted I am not sure I could trust future representative and senators to hold the line at $15,000. Somehow they will find a way to change it to their advantage and make us feel like they are looking out for our interests.

As a passing note, my sympathies to the residents of California if the governor has his way about providing health care for all children, including illegal aliens. You are going to get hosed with taxes.

Here are some terms you should know about because they are part of our current system and will be until you and I can convince enough Americans to help us fix health care in this country.

**COBRA** is a federal program that allows employees to remain on their company health plans for up to 18 months after leaving the employer by paying the insurance premiums out of pocket. The system is designed to prevent people who are between jobs from experiencing a lapse in coverage. NOTE: This would not be an issue under my health care proposal.

**HIPAA** is an Act of Congress that gives people the right to insurance coverage from any provider as long as they have been covered by a group policy in the previous 63 days. Even people with serious illnesses must receive coverage from any carrier if they can pay the premium costs, which are not regulated by HIPAA. HIPAA is also a Privacy Act regarding the privacy of health information.

**Managed Care** (such as an HMO or PPO) offers significant coverage at a lower cost in premiums and deductibles. However, the plans can be inflexible and some visits, medications and treatments ***may not be approved by the insurer***. (Do you want insurance companies making decisions on your health?)

## DOCTORS

When I started working as a registered pharmacist I looked upon doctors (physicians) as God like, because of their stature in the medical profession, as well as the community. To become a doctor required more years of education than most any other profession, additional years as an intern and a lot of money. When a doctor completed his residency and could open his own practice he was certainly entitled to the financial rewards that would come to him.

Every community I was aware of was always looking for and inviting new doctors to settle in their community. Usually a doctor did not move from one community to another because they were firmly entrenched within that community by their patient base. Every doctor in a community was busy seeing as many patients as possible every day because they were in demand. In addition to seeing patients in their office, they always had patients in the hospital and would see them early every morning before beginning work at the office. Then there were the emergency calls at night and on weekends. When a doctor took a well deserved vacation they had arrangements with other doctors to cover patients while out of town. There was really no such thing as a day off because if he was in town everyone knew it and calls would come.

This was the medical profession I grew up with, doctors being overworked but very well respected and in almost every case making as much money as they would ever need, provided they could find some time to enjoy their wealth. Even though they were considered wealthy, they carried large accounts receivable and did a lot of "free" work for those unable to pay them. Their professional oath required them to not turn away those in need.

This face of medicine began to change for doctors, pharmacies and hospitals when the government enacted Medicare/Medicaid legislation. Suddenly doctors became even busier when the previously indigent patients learned they could get "free" medical services such as office visits, treatments, prescriptions and more. They flooded doctor offices "demanding" service. The previously overworked doctors were now even busier and I think it took years for them to realize what was happening. They were enjoying an extra source of revenue from the government and that probably made the situation reasonably tolerable.

A simple fifteen minute office visit with one of these Medicaid recipients required much more time to fill out paperwork in order to receive the money. As time went on, not only did the paperwork require more and more time to fill out, but it was even more time before the doctor actually received the money.

I am sure there were days when a doctor wondered why he chose his profession. It was not unusual for a doctor to call in a prescription, and than take a few minutes to talk with me. I think this was a temporary and relaxing outlet for some of his frustrations and I always enjoyed these brief visits. Dealing with sick people continuously was bad enough, but I know first hand how difficult some customers/patients can be. Maybe it was my imagination, but it seemed as if those people who received free services were the most demanding. I am convinced that socialism of any kind will never work because of attitudes like this. Whatever the arguments for socialism, human nature with our innate spirit to be free and to utilize all the gifts God gave us dooms socialism. But we must be continually vigilant against those who would use socialism to control us.

Looking back I think doctors went along with the system thrust upon them much longer than they should have. This probably occurred because there were no clear cut solutions. Doctors were trained to be "doctors", to save lives and many lacked the business acumen required to find creative alternatives. They saw their insurance costs skyrocket because of over aggressive lawyers looking for an easy buck. One solution was to return to school and become specialists or surgeons. This solution was probably necessary to increase their fees as much as to control insurance costs.

Whatever the reasons, the changes have created confusion within the medical industry. Patients, not knowing exactly what was wrong, were confused about which specialist to see. The family doctor, a general practitioner, virtually disappeared, coincidentally about the same time independent pharmacies began falling by the wayside. Let us understand that these changes within the medical industry also created a vacuum for patients who wondered where they could go to receive the advice, or counseling about their condition as they had in the past. As an independent pharmacist I was often the initial source of information for customers "not feeling well" and wondering what to do. Through education and experience, we could recognize if an illness required more than an over-the-counter solution and we could quickly recommend they seek medical treatment from a doctor or hospital. This type of service is not readily available in today's environment.

Not only has the government adversely affected a doctor's environment, but lawyers and insurance companies have also contributed to complicating a doctor's life. To me lawyers are like a hawk always vigilant for an easy meal or opportunity. Morally speaking, I have a problem with holding doctors accountable to perfection. They are very well trained and dedicated to serving those in need, but within our society there are those individuals looking for an easy buck when a doctor misdiagnoses. These people are generally the less educated of us, usually not affluent and when an opportunity comes for a big payday as promised by ambulance chasing lawyers, they cannot resist.

I know from experience that most people have difficulty describing their discomfort and more importantly do not always tell the doctor everything he/she did that may have contributed to their problem. If in a hospital, a patient may be unconscious and unable to say anything. I remember vividly my father-in-law passed away in the hospital emergency room when the doctor did not suspect an aneurysm which burst and he bled to death internally. Treated expeditiously, it was a very treatable condition. I can see where it would be easy to blame the doctor and avow to the world he was incompetent, but it never occurred to us to bring a mal-practice law suit against the doctor.

Faced with this kind of scrutiny what is a doctor to do? Well, he orders every test he can think of so as to cover his "you know what". These tests are not inexpensive and the patient or their insurance plan must pay out many unnecessary dollars. In today's environment, I can just visualize the lawyer lurking, or hovering, and rubbing his hand together in anticipation. It is unfortunate that we live in such a litigious society. The truth is that doctors make mistakes just like every other human does and they did not make a mistake on purpose. If they are indeed less than competent their practice will succeed or fail accordingly.

Just as the government and lawyers have caused problems for doctors, insurance companies have also contributed and are not without their share of blame. Insurance companies usually determine the fees doctors will receive from them for their services. As a result, doctors can get kind of "creative" with insurance claims. They routinely place an inflated fee for a service because they know the insurance company is going to discount the claim and pay the doctor what the insurance company thinks is fair.

As an example, I have seen a chiropractor for a back problem and when I initially saw him he would charge a fee of $30 for a visit. During the visit it was always the same treatment. I would get on the table and he would check out my back, then it was off to the roller bed for relaxation. Every time I went it was the same and it was $30. When I became eligible for Medicare and supplemental insurance the fee I paid decreased to $15 per visit and he billed the insurance company for the services. The insurance company sent me copies of the bills and I noticed they were being billed $95 for my visit, but they were remitting to the doctor $29.

Now, I want to be clear I am not accusing the doctor of taking advantage of the situation which increased his total received fees from $30 per visit to $44. I am very comfortable with understanding that he probably paid someone the extra $14 just to fill out the paperwork he had to file with the insurance company. This real life situation identifies one reason health care costs have increased so much.

This example is indicative of how all health care providers have to deal with insurance companies and the effect of this game carries over and affects people who do not have insurance. Our politicians have declared that health care providers cannot charge the government a different or higher fee than they would charge paying customers who pay with cash. As a result, insurance companies have the same rule, so now cash customers get soaked even though they pay cash. The government also now scrutinizes doctors who serve both cash customers and Medicare customers to make sure they are being "fair".

It is no wonder there is a shortage of doctors, because fewer people are entering the medical profession and I think it is very indicative of how and why socialism does not work.

The good news is that doctors seem to be changing the way they practice medicine and I hope and pray they have not started too late to help stave off the ravages of socialism. I sense a move by doctors to a more direct approach to the practice of medicine. It seems doctors are preparing for the day when government and insurance companies no longer control their livelihood.

Through the limited research I did for this book, and casual reading, I discovered there are businesses out there that are teaching doctors how to communicate better with patients. In school doctors were taught medicine and not much focus on communication skills and business principles. Remembering back to my early days in pharmacy, doctors were always busy and traditionally that has not changed very much. Doctors are beginning to realize if they are to compete successfully, they must be able to communicate, especially if the medical profession moves more to a free enterprise environment.

The new environment developing is for doctors to sell access to patients willing to pay for unlimited visits with the doctor. I have seen annual fees of $500 to $3,500 for an individual and $1,800 to $7,500 for a family. These fees are just for access and not covered by insurance. This type of medical practice may be called "boutique" or "concierge" medicine. Patients can expect extended visits with the doctor that may last 15 or 20 minutes instead of 5 minutes. Patients will also have access to the doctor 24 hours per day. Since the fees are for time only, patients will pay for any services they need. Some clinics do not even accept insurance covered patients.

Practices that have initiated this type of medical practice are finding that doctors can now work normal 3 to 5 day weeks and still have time to spend with their families. As one might guess, there are some critics to this approach to practicing medicine

Here in my home state I know of a chain of medical clinics that charge an annual fee for access and some service. Their approach is they accept no insurance. Individuals pay an annual fee plus registration for unlimited office visits and an annual physical. The annual rate for a family of any size is a flat fee with the same benefits. If additional services are needed they are paid for by the patient. This "chain" of clinics is throughout the state and growing rapidly. Since not everyone qualifies for insurance or can afford insurance, these clinics are signing up patients through their own marketing efforts and allowing insurance agencies to offer this unique plan as an alternative to traditional "health insurance plans".

Another type of medical practice that seems to be gaining in popularity is called "supermarket medicine". The name fits because they are located in supermarkets, especially those multi-tasking centers that also include eye clinics, blood pressure stands and pharmacies.

My sense is these approaches to the practice of medicine and others similar to it are the future of medicine and in the conclusion of this book I will show how doctors, hospitals and pharmacy can unite to make overall medical practice a win, win situation for everyone and especially the citizens needing medical care.

## DRUG COMPANIES & DRUGS

Drug companies and the services they provide are a big part of our health care system and it would be helpful for America to understand just how big. I start this discussion by stating that drug companies play a vital role in advancing the capabilities of treating diseases in our society. But let us first understand that drug companies are driven by profit. Drug companies are not part of government and thank God for that. By necessity drug companies are engaging in activities that I have a problem with and these activities also go a long way to confusing the public.

There is a lot of confusion about drug prices today, because we hear much about purchasing mail order prescriptions from Canada or Mexico because of lower prices. When I started my career in pharmacy and purchased drugs to stock my pharmacy, I thought I was paying the same price other institutions were paying. When it came to dispensing prescriptions the only competition I had was from other pharmacies. Hospitals had pharmacies, but they were for internal dispensing of drugs for hospital inpatients and really not considered competition. Super markets had not yet gotten into having pharmacies inside the market for the convenience of their customers. There were no mail order pharmacies. The result was a pretty level playing field when it came to drug prices.

Today, drug companies are forced to sell drugs probably through a bidding process to government institutions, hospitals, large volume mail order outlets, internationally to whichever outlet is responsible for that country's health care system and the list goes on. Keep in mind that drug companies are still driven by the bottom line net profit for their stock holders. As a result there will be very uneven pricing for their products. When I was still in pharmacy, it was independent pharmacies that paid exorbitant prices for drugs. The current feeling by most citizens and politicians is that the government needs to control prices and I can think of no greater mistake.

Have you ever thought about what it takes to develop one new drug? These companies spend millions (more than likely billions) of dollars on research to develop compounds that treat illnesses. I do not know the exact numbers but it probably takes the development of thousands of compounds to find one drug. These compounds have to be tested and evaluated for effectiveness, dosage, delivery methods, stability, and by the way, which illness a compound will treat. The drug company derives no revenue until they have something to market and then the government determines when the drug is ready and gives its blessing to the released drug.

Now the drug company must make sure the drug will be prescribed by doctors and of course marketing costs are very high. Every step of the way has a cost to the drug manufacturer and the total cost plus a profit needs to be recouped in a given period of time. Why a given period of time you ask? Because patent laws only protect the originator of the drug from competition for a government determined period of time before it becomes available as a generic drug.

Here is where our self serving politicians pander to the public when they, "in the interest of reducing drug costs", shorten the patent life so it becomes a generic where competition drives costs down. The window to recoup development costs is much smaller and the result is high drug costs to the public.

But this is just one of the problems for drug companies. A new drug may find its way slowly into the health care system because they are usually very expensive and to find its way onto a formulary list is very rare. For a new drug to be on any treatment formulary, it will have to treat some new illness. Maybe this is why today illnesses have creative names like "acid reflux disease" and "ED (erectile dysfunction)", and "ADD (attention deficit disorder)" that were not considered as illnesses several years ago.

Let's take a humorous look at these ridiculous illnesses. "Acid reflux" is a result of over eating food that is probably well seasoned and spicy. Eating less and carrying a roll of some antacid will fix the problem, but no, commercials have identified this illness and there is a "prescription" drug available, so off we go to the doctor. Then there is the natural occurring male disorder of ED that occurs with age and weight gain. You know, sometimes life happens. This brings me to my favorite "manufactured illness" that occurs mostly in children called "ADD (attention deficit disorder). The names implies that children have trouble concentrating at school and when teachers notice this "illness" they send a note home informing the parents that their child suffers from ADD and treatment is recommended. I have a hard time believing that doctors go along with this hoax, but some do. Children grow and some have more energy than others and this is considered an illness? A little discipline and more PE (physical education) at school would solve the problem.

We were talking about drug companies and their need to market their new products. A new drug has just been developed and it can only be sold on a prescription, but if a doctor is unaware of this brand new drug he cannot be expected to prescribe it to patients who may need it. So how do they solve this problem? Well they buy advertising on TV and develop feel good ads that show a disheveled person needing this new drug and by the end of the commercial they are dancing and prancing around. Some unsuspecting person watching one of these commercials will suddenly think he is afflicted with this illness and off to the doctor he goes to get his prescription. This practice is very clever and dangerous and I cringe when I see them on TV.

These "direct-to-consumer" ads for prescription drugs are more emotional than educational and as a society we must remember that prescription drugs are not like purchasing candy. With consumers going to doctors and pressuring the doctor to prescribe these drugs I can only see problems. If you make a wrong decision about a prescription drug, it could have very serious adverse effects. I heard about a February, 2006, Consumer Reports survey that stated 78 percent of primary care physicians said their patients ask them for drugs they have seen advertised on TV. Further, the survey suggested that 67 percent of physicians concede that they sometimes grant their patients' requests.

Interestingly, only the United States and New Zealand allow these direct-to-consumer ads and New Zealand is considering an outright ban. I cannot find anything written about another consequence associated with these ads but it is called "branding". I think the drug companies want their products branded should the drug eventually find its way to the non-prescription, over-the-counter market where theirs' will be the most recognized brand.

There is more evidence that drug price controls will not work and will have dangerous consequences. After the November 2006 elections, the new leaders in congress announced they would move to allow the government to negotiate directly with pharmaceutical companies to obtain lower drug prices for Medicare patients. Supposedly this plan looked a lot like the system currently in Italy, where drug prices are among the lowest in Europe. Drugs in Europe average about 60 percent less than in the United States. Even as U.S. prices rose, Italian drug prices decreased by 5 percent last year. Remember my earlier discussion about how drug companies have various prices but still maintain a healthy bottom line? Who do you think is paying more so that Italy can have lower prices? Surely it is not possible to lower the costs to manufacture drugs just because a government entity "demands" lower prices. If this were true, every business school in the world should give a refund to all of their former students, because this is not how any business model works.

At first glance the Italian model might seem an enviable model for America to follow. Before we get too excited let us look at the Italian system to see if it really is a paradise. According to **Alberto Mingardi**, a director of the *Istituto Bruno Leoni*, an Italian free-market think tank, the Italian system is more like a quagmire of red tape, than a health care paradise.

Italy's lower drug prices are the product of government price controls because the state purchases nearly 60 percent of the nation's prescription drugs. Supposedly the state negotiates prices directly with drug companies and controls such a disproportionate share of the market it in effect dictates drug prices.

In Italy, these price controls have created a number of problems. First, these price controls distort the laws of supply and demand. Because of the country's *artificially* low drug prices, demand for drugs is artificially high, much higher than it would be under free-market conditions. There is a valuable lesson here! Just because the government of Italy has successfully forced down drug prices does not mean they have reduced overall health care spending. As a result they have experienced a spike, or increased demand for drugs by the populace and health care spending has skyrocketed, growing nearly 68 percent between 1995 and 2003.

There is a basic law in physics; for every action there is comparable and equal reaction. The government in Italy made a bad decision to create drug price controls and it led to an increased demand for drugs. The result is Italy's health care is suffering both in quality of care and the financial costs. The Italian government has attempted to save money by adopting reimbursement policies that favor certain drugs over others. Unfortunately, the most innovative products often aren't considered reimbursable by the government precisely because they are the most expensive. This is a great system if all you need is an antibiotic. If you are hoping to avoid something like open-heart surgery, when there is a miracle drug available to alleviate the health problem, the system can be a nightmare.

Italians are lacking more than just choice in cutting-edge drugs. They also lack information. According to a recent survey, more than 50 percent of Italy's patients believe that the national (government) health care service cannot even supply adequate information about treatments and drugs. There is more!! The economy is also harmed. It simply is not profitable for drug companies to invent cures in Italy; price controls have decimated Italy's drug industry. Today, not one of the world's 50 largest drug manufacturers has its headquarters in Italy, even though the country is the world's seventh largest economy. Most drug and bio-technology companies are outside the borders of Italy and there are only a few thousand workers in Italy's entire drug industry which means these workers are a favorite target of the country's politicians. The politicians can rail against the drug industry with little political downside.

Pardon me for thinking, but the politicians in Italy created the problem by pandering to the citizenry and pompously creating price controls. Now it is not working and they blame the drug company workers. This sounds a whole lot like what is happening in this country when our politicians promise health care. What they are really promising is "socialized medicine". They can give health care a sexier name like "universal health care", but it would still be socialized medicine.

Here is a fact for all Americans to remember. This socialized form of health care has no recorded success anywhere in the world and never will. Please, remember the bottom line of what has happened in Italy with health care. The Italian government has deprived its citizens of the best care without reducing health care spending and they have deprived the country of what could be a vibrant sector of the economy. Bringing health care closer to our shores, we could look at Canada and you would see the same problems as we have seen in Italy.

There is a bright side for us! Currently in the U.S., government health care spending is roughly 20 percent of the national budget. If we could be successful in preventing the disaster of socialized medicine in this country, the government could really reduce our taxes. This would boost even more the best economy the world has ever known. Think of how much more you and I could prosper and provide for our children.

Let us also be realistic, preventing creeping socialism and big government will not happen unless you and I demand of our politicians a halt to growing governmental intrusion in our lives. This will not be easy and will not happen unless all of us do our part to educate ourselves in the dangers of taking medications.

When I started my career in pharmacy I was very naïve about drug use. Having just graduated from college with a degree in pharmacy, I had been trained in how drugs worked and how lives were lengthening because of advances in modern medicine. I never really gave much thought in those days as to how drugs could affect individuals who abused them. After all, doctors were prescribing drugs to their patients and my job depended on filling as many prescriptions as I could. It was almost hypnotic to think I was "helping" people.

It was not until I had a few years of experience under my belt that I began to question why people had to take so many drugs. The more I studied the causes and effects of taking drugs by interacting with my customers; I began to understand just how much some of my customers depended on drugs to get through their day. I began to realize a lot of my customers needed more than just symptomatic relief of aches and pains. They were really hooked on the euphoria drugs gave them for a few hours. We think an individual can only get hooked on "narcotics", but customers were getting hooked by habits. The habit of liking the euphoria they received when they popped that pill.

During this time I came to a conclusion that was scary and I will admit up front there was no formal study on my part. The conclusion came from experience that about 70 percent of the drugs prescribed really did not need to be prescribed. Even my years away from an active practice of pharmacy have not changed my conclusion in any way and today the conclusion may even be that there is more unnecessary drug use.

For the most part I have been talking about "legend" drugs meaning they can only be sold with a prescription from a doctor. There are large numbers of drugs sold through pharmacies, supermarkets or mass merchandisers commonly called OTC, or over-the-counter drugs. Many of these products were at one time legend drugs and became so widely used that the government allowed their sale without a prescription. The assumption by most Americans is that if it can be sold without a prescription, it is safe to take. This assumption is very wrong!

Let's look at one decongestant drug with a generic name of pseudoephedrine, sold for many years under the name of Sudafed and various generic trade names. This drug is also an ingredient in many combination products taken to treat congestion and runny noses caused by allergies, cold, flu, etc. The most common side effects of this drug are dryness of the mouth and stimulation (a sense of a lot of energy). So, while this drug gave general relief to the discomforts of congestion and runny noses, the stimulation also helped offset the drowsiness caused by taking antihistamines when they were a part of these combination products, as is usually the case.

Here are the possible problems with taking products like this. One, the antihistamines cause drowsiness and driving a vehicle could be dangerous, especially if one gets sleepy. If alcohol is ingested while taking antihistamines the side effects might be potentiated, so the user may feel drunk or sleepy. Two, there is the stimulation caused when taking pseudoephedrine. After all, pseudoephedrine is a derivative of ephedrine, widely used to bring people out of stupors caused by shock or reaction to other drugs. Long ago college students learned they could more easily study all night by taking this "safe" over-the-counter product. Three, the decongestant effects of these products, can also cause the body to become dehydrated. Dehydration comes from not drinking enough water, especially while taking the medications and the side effects of dehydration might be muscle cramping just to mention one. Dehydration is dangerous and way too many of us do not drink as much water on a daily basis as we should. Four, the stimulation caused by pseudoephedrine may also elevate one's blood pressure and we all have heard how dangerous that can be.

Here is the point where the story gets interesting. Illegal drug dealers learned to manufacture methamphetamine from pseudoephedrine. Law enforcement people are always on the look out for "meth" houses because this is really big business for illegal drug dealers. When the sale of all over-the-counter products containing pseudoephedrine skyrocketed and law enforcement officials finally figured things out, the sale of these products became somewhat restricted. Now, these products are kept behind the prescription counter and the pharmacist decides whether the customer really needs this product or not. By the way, methamphetamine was widely sold on a prescription only basis, because it was a big time stimulant, but it also reduced the taker's appetite. This, of course, meant the product was desired for weight loss.

See what can happen by taking these seemingly safe products. Other widely sold and consumed products are the many pain killers. Used for headaches, sore joints and muscles and any other conditions of discomfort. A lot of people I know have some "headache" pills handy, such as in their car, purse or briefcase and they will not hesitate to "pop" some themselves, or even worse, pass them out like candy to friends.

The possible dangerous "side" effects of pretty much all pain killers are just about the same and, while there could be exceptions, they remain consistent. If I had a headache my first thought would be, what caused it? What about my daily routine is different enough to trigger a headache? Am I under stress, was I in the hot sun too much, have I drunk enough water, have I drunk too much of something else, what about my routine caused the headache? When I was a pharmacist and a customer asked for a recommendation, I would inquire of them what they thought triggered the headache. Many times customers did not know or would not tell me what may have caused the headache, they just wanted relief

Besides temporary relief from the headache or pain, what else happens? Most of these products, when taken, cause irritation or lesions within the intestinal tract. To counteract this problem many people also take chalky-white products called antacids. Once a drug is absorbed by the body it can cause destruction of some blood cells and/or interact adversely with other medications. These drugs may also cause constipation or diarrhea.

Besides all the possible side effects the biggest problem when taking these products is they may only mask the real problem of what caused the headache in the first place. The cause may need more treatment than the symptoms.

Now, my fellow Americans, here is the real scary part! You and I will never be successful in reducing our need for expensive health insurance unless we become more responsible in taking drugs, by first reducing consumption of drugs, and thus reducing dependence on them. That's right! I am suggesting the solution lies largely in our hands. The alternative will be government run socialized health care programs that take away our freedoms and make us "wards of the state". In addition, we must make sure our politicians understand the potential ravages of socialized medicine. Do not be confused if the politicians call this concept "universal health care" to make it sound better. It is all socialism!

Just for the record, as I am writing this book I do not take medications. The only possible exception would be that I take two aspirin tablets every night with my regular regimen of vitamins and my use of aspirin goes back a long way. I believe that aspirin keeps my blood vessels clear, plus aspirin is a mild muscle relaxant so I sleep better. I tell you this so you understand I am not suggesting you do anything I would not do. You may ask if I would take medications if prescribed by a physician and the answer is a very qualified maybe. Short of an act of congress the doctor would have to be very convincing for me to take drugs.

Let us first agree that our bodies have a marvelous capacity for healing if allowed to do so. Medications should be given only to help the body in its healing capacity. Everyone should strive to improve their health to the point that medications become unnecessary. When I started this book I was grossly overweight because I like to eat. Since I do not smoke, food tastes good. And since I had no apparent physical problems the down side to being overweight was I had no more clothes to wear, my belly stuck out, walking upstairs caused shortness of breath, and I waddled when I walked. My blood pressure was probably high and besides looking like a walking blimp, I was not happy with the situation.

A friend of mine visited one day and told me he had lost 60 pounds with one of the weight loss programs and he felt great. I decided I was going to lose weight and I did not need a doctor to tell me to do this. In other words, I was lucky to be healthy enough I could make the decision and not have to live with someone else telling me I had to lose weight. Remember, as stated in the introduction to this book, I want to look good when you and I have a chance to meet.

Well I am all of 6 feet tall and when I started this book I weighted 290 pounds. Four and a half months later I had lost forty plus pounds on my way to a goal weight of 180 pounds. Has it been easy? The answer is a very definite no!! But the rewards are great because I am feeling so much better and I have more energy.

I do not tell you this to brag. I tell you this because if I could do this of my own free will, you can work at healing what you need to and here is a most important fact

that you can relate to: I DID NOT NEED THE
GOVERNMENT TO TELL ME TO LOSE WEIGHT!!

Sincerely speaking, I cannot overstate the importance
of staying away from taking drugs unless it is a matter of
life or death. I will not go so far as to say we are a nation
of drug users because the term "drug users" brings up
connotation that may be inappropriate. However, adding
two letters to the term "drug users" changes the term to
one I think is more appropriate. Add the letters "a" and
"b" to drug users and you have "drug abusers" and I am
sad to say that I think the term fits.

It is so easy to be convinced that drugs can be a safe
solution to whatever ailment we have with the sexy TV
commercials, readily available products and lack of
education about the dangers of taking drugs.

As a conclusion to this chapter we need to realize that
drug companies may suffer reduced sales as society adjusts
to the concept of better health, but they will adjust and
prosper over time in a free-enterprise economy that will
benefit everyone. If Americans become less dependent on
drugs, our health care costs will come down and it is very
important for us to convince politicians they cannot buy
our votes with the hollow promises of universal health
care.

## PHARMACY

At the time I started my career in pharmacy, this profession played an important role in the overall health care system and we will look at some of the ways. With the advent of government programs and the growth of the insurance industry's role, the evolution of the health care system has brought about the virtual elimination of the role pharmacy should play. Hopefully in the future, pharmacy will once again have a vibrant role.

I graduated from the university with a BS in Pharmacy degree and went to work in a retail pharmacy. At that time pharmacists were not only well known in the community, but were well respected professionals. Pharmacist played a prominent role in the community as they participated in professional organizations such as Rotary Clubs, Lions Clubs and more. Often the pharmacist would run for city or county offices, serve on hospital boards or some such capacity to give back to the community.

When the government programs started, such as Medicare and Medicaid, pharmacists were none too happy when we were told how the programs would work and how little we would be paid for stocking the inventory, doing the required paperwork for reimbursement and filling the prescriptions (with all the risks and responsibilities that went with filling prescriptions). Pharmacists were told to accept the programs or the government would open their own pharmacies to dispense welfare prescriptions, so like sheep, we went along.

Today the independent retail pharmacy has disappeared. Independents have been replaced by chain pharmacies that sell foods, gifts, photo developing and more to make money because insurance companies have taken all of the profit out of filling prescriptions. It has been my experience through the years that "chain pharmacies" do not offer any competent level of customer service. This may be more a result of the system than by intentional design. With very little, or no, profit in filling prescriptions, chain pharmacists must fill a large number of prescriptions to justify their salary. Patient counseling has become a voluminous mountain of pre-printed paperwork handed to customers with their prescriptions. The dispensed prescription vial today looks more like NASCAR vehicles with many colored advertisements painted on them, than a professional product that may hold the patients health. Many of the warning labels are generic enough to apply to a large percentage of all drugs and thus, warnings become insignificant to patients.

The part pharmacy should play in a successful health care system should not be minimized, so let's look at the role pharmacy played prior to government intervention. Very few pharmacies were computerized, yet we were to be aware of possible drug interactions that could harm our customers. Often it was easier for pharmacists to keep up with characteristics of a new drug as they came on market, than for the doctors. Because our inventory reflected all the drugs local doctors would use, we often heard the same product spiel from drug company representatives that the doctor heard. This was part of an important role in the health care system because doctors were often too busy to see the drug company representative and hear the presentation. They may have heard or read about this new drug and if the indications would help one of their patients they wanted to use it. If the doctor or patient had questions, the pharmacists were convenient and available to answer those questions.

Because doctors were always kept very busy they really took little time to explain directions to their patients, clarifying how the drug should be taken, drug warnings and possible side effects. This responsibility often fell to the pharmacist. It was not unusual for pharmacists to actually explain why the customer/patient was taking the drug(s). Doctors and pharmacist were a team and each played a vital role in an individual's health. Our team was not much different than the doctor/hospital team, everyone had an important role.

Then the government got involved by creating Medicare and Medicaid and things changed dramatically. These programs offered free doctor visits, free treatment services and free prescriptions for the "poor". As you can imagine it did not take long for them to figure out how the system worked. Doctor's offices became even more crowded and paperwork for doctors, pharmacists and hospitals created a whole new level of what I call harassment, but should more accurately be termed additional office expense. But if we wanted to get paid, we had to complete the forms.

The number of people that qualified for the "free" programs turned out to be larger than government estimates expected and this should not surprise anyone. Government expenditures grew rapidly each year and politicians were not about to end a program no matter how flawed, thus was born "socialized medicine". These programs did two things that rapidly changed the face of health care as we had known it. Doctors increased their revenues while pharmacies took a big hit and the result was that independent retail pharmacies began to disappear.

Some of the blame for the demise of independent retail pharmacies, in addition to reduced fees, was attributed to discriminate pricing of drugs by the wholesalers and manufacturers. In other words a retail pharmacy was going to pay more for Valium than a hospital would be required to pay. This was totally unfair and we actually learned that government facilities and large institutions were paying less for these same drugs. It was an uneven playing field and to make things worse, the independent pharmacies just happened to be where the "welfare recipients" went to have their prescriptions filled.

It should be of no surprise that with people standing in line for these "free" government paid health services, the actual program costs zoomed far above government estimates. Cutbacks had to be implemented or the programs would go bankrupt. Gee, what a surprise! Yet another failed government program was in the making and no one should be surprised when I tell you that our elected politicians could not let this happen. Besides pouring more of our tax dollars at the problem, cuts in services were gradually implemented to alleviate the financial burden on the government.

One of the first cuts was to limit how many prescriptions one recipient could receive each month. Another favorite cost cutter was to routinely reduce the fees pharmacists and doctors could charge for services to "welfare recipients". They also demanded that any discounts a pharmacy received for paying bills on time were passed on to the government. It was illegal for a pharmacist to substitute a generic drug on a prescription where a generic existed for a more expensive brand name drug. However, for "welfare recipients" this illegality was actually encouraged and "required" UNLESS a doctor wrote on the prescription "brand name only". How practical was this? Doctors were busy and really could not have cared less about taking the time to write something else on a prescription.

One other restriction developed was to create a "formulary" of drugs that would be covered or paid for by the government programs. In other words, some patient illnesses are not treated or if treated, face limitations. Here is a "modern day" example of how the regulation of drugs and treatments can become an infringement on a patient's privacy. The church I belong to has an outreach ministry that provides counseling for people with emotional and mental difficulties. These difficulties may be temporary or permanent. The center has a fund to help those who cannot pay, but if a patient is covered by health insurance they cannot use the insurance unless the doctor diagnoses the patient as "insane" and writes the word "insane" on the insurance form.

Put yourself in this situation and ask if you would be willing to think of yourself as insane for the rest of your life.

Another situation that government programs fostered was to encourage welfare mothers to give birth to more children out of wedlock. Each additional child increased that mother's monthly income from the government. "Fathers need not apply!"

I spent twenty years in retail pharmacy and thoroughly enjoyed helping people understand their health issues and helping them get well. As time went on, however, I began to understand how things worked. At that time, I owned a pharmacy and had about $60,000 invested in inventory just in the prescription department. I could not sell any of this $60,000 unless I had a "permission" slip from a doctor called a prescription. It was a constant challenge to keep the inventory down, yet complete enough to fill prescriptions. In addition to this financial burden I was required to keep records, be knowledgeable about drug usage and warnings, possible interactions and more.

As time went on, I began to pay attention to effects drugs had on people when they took them. This was a small town and we knew and were friends with our customers. I could recall from memory all the drugs a family took and I was available for questions or counseling of their needs. Conversations with customers might include the upcoming football game, weather, and more, but the conversations also would be about what the drug was really for, clarity of instructions and more. These were opportunities to learn more about the real effects drugs were having on customers I knew.

The more I talked to customers, the more I became somewhat of a student about how drugs alter one's body and/or mind. One of the most popular prescriptions I filled was for birth control pills. Birth control pills are hormones or closely related drugs that tricked the female's body into not allowing pregnancy as long as they took them. But God did not create us to be the same as everyone else and in this case women could respond differently to a given drug. I will not list all the different moods a woman can have, but these popular drugs literally could change one's personality. A wife might become less cordial after getting married and taking birth control pills did not help the situation and in fact often exacerbated the situation.

I never really paid much attention to this phenomenon until the husbands came in with a prescription for an anti-depressant drug. Being a student of drug use it was logical to try and understand what was happening here. The first time I questioned this, involved a family I knew well and the husband was too young to need "anti-depressants". He related to me how his wife had gotten too hard to live with and to save the marriage he needed help. As a friend I suggested he allow his wife to stop taking birth control pills and consider some other form of contraception. Within ninety days, the family relationship was back to normal and needless to say I was somewhat of a "hero" to them. As time went on I was able to counsel others with much the same results.

The more time I spent in pharmacy the more I learned about the consequences of taking drugs. Another of my customers had been faithful to my business for almost fifteen years and one day she came walking to my prescription counter at a very slow pace. She stopped in front of my counter and plopped two new prescriptions on the counter. As I greeted her and inquired how she was feeling she told me she had no energy. I flippantly suggested she should exercise more. She then told me she could not even walk to the mailbox without sitting on the curb and resting.

As I looked at her list of active prescriptions I asked if the doctor wanted her to discontinue taking any of them. She answered that she "guessed not" because the doctor did not say anything to her about that. I took the opportunity to suggest to her that she might be taking too many drugs and that it was no wonder she felt the way she did. I also explained to her the dangers of suddenly discontinuing taking any medications she had been taking for awhile. To suddenly stop taking medications could be hazardous without supervision. She then asked what I would suggest. I mentioned a well respected clinic I knew of about 150 miles away that I had heard good things about and suggested she call for an appointment. The next day she came in and told me she had an appointment at the clinic, but her local doctor would not give her a copy of her medical records. While I am not a lawyer, I knew the doctor had to release her medical records and when she went back the doctor handed them over to her.

Three weeks later this lady walked into my pharmacy with a smile on her face and a bounce in her step. She excitedly told me how successful the clinic had been in altering her medications. This episode really got me thinking about another line of work because not only was the doctor mad at me, I received very few prescriptions written by him from that time on.

I have shared these experiences because they serve to show how starved people are for information and help in making health decisions. At the same time, I began to re-thinking my life in pharmacy. Technically I may have stepped over the line by offering advice like that because whether a patient takes, or does not take, a medication is really a decision for a licensed doctor. But the more I studied "why" prescriptions are written I realized that the most successful doctors wrote the most prescriptions. Remember, this was pre-government health care and a time when health care was closer to what I call "free enterprise" business. Without any statistics to back up my thinking, I have always felt that seventy percent of prescriptions written did not need to be written.

The citizenry is not blameless in this because I also learned that when people visited their doctor and paid for that office visit, they expected new prescriptions and were unhappy if they did not receive them.

Let's not overlook the tremendous amount of money that can be wasted when purchasing large quantities of drugs via mail-order pharmacies. By law prescription drugs are not returnable for any credit if unused. In order for mail-order pharmacies to be efficient they will only dispense drugs in at least three-month quantities. At times a doctor will ask a patient not to continue taking a drug and unused quantities are wasted. I am impressed with modern day Wal-Mart pharmacies. They will dispense a one month quantity of any generic prescription for about $4, and this makes a lot of sense. It also should show everyone that free enterprise works.

I hope this chapter has successfully demonstrated how independent pharmacies have a place in our overall health care needs. The pharmacies of old served a useful purpose, but they have virtually disappeared from our modern health care system and they are being sorely missed. I cannot forecast the future but in my blueprint for fixing health care in this country I see the return of this profession.

## HOSPITALS

Hospitals are an integral part of an overall health care program and serve as a base for doctors. A doctor may have an office for his practice away from the hospital, but after hours and on weekends more often than not a call to a doctor will be answered by a hospital switchboard. In addition to serving as a focal point for the doctors in their community, hospitals provide facilities for surgical procedures, recovery rooms for temporary patient stays, nursing help, and much more. There is no way to separate the hospital/doctor relationship but let us understand the part hospitals play.

If someone faces a medical emergency and shows up at a hospital expecting treatment they will receive no treatment unless a doctor is brought into the occasion. In no way should anyone expect to set up residence in a hospital room, it is not a hotel. Even those unfortunate people who need long term care and assistance after their physical condition is stabilized are often transferred to facilities set up for the longer term and specialized care needs of patients.

It is helpful to know that there are many types of hospitals, but any one hospital will be there to serve the needs of the community in which they reside. Smaller communities have very different hospitals than those found in larger communities or cities. In the small communities a hospital may be called upon to treat everyone that shows up in need of service. If the medical needs are more severe the patient may be transferred to another hospital better equipped to meet that particular need.

Hospitals in larger communities may be specialty hospitals emphasizing treatments of cancer, heart problems, psychological needs, pediatrics, or they may be a "teaching" facility. Regardless of their size or treatment focus, most hospitals are subsidized by local, state or national governmental entities. This is not the best situation, but in today's health care concept it is necessary to have facilities where people can go for treatment, but we need to begin changing the situation. There is a better way and I hope you and I can be successful in changing the "system".

In the process of organizing my thoughts for this book, I did an internet search for "hospital trends" to see if changes are being made since it has been a few years since I was active with hospitals. The message at the bottom of the first screen told me there were fifteen million articles about this topic. To be honest I did not read all of them, but there was enough information in the ones I did read for me to see there are some trends developing that could get us on the right tract.

In addition to trends there are websites you can go to and learn more about the cost and quality of common medical procedures, but you can also get confused because there may be 150, more or less, acute care hospitals in an average size state. We can learn how many people received a certain treatment, what the posted prices are for a medical treatment and much more information in such a large quantity you can get "information overload".

Other helpful information may not appear on a website such as the hospital's specific numbers on patient mortality, infections or the rate of patient readmissions. Prices shown will be inflated "insurance" prices, and remember that not everyone has insurance. You may also find a hospital score, and as I understand accreditation, each hospital has a "rating" or "score", but the methodology of the accreditation process may skew the score. The website I looked at for the State of Georgia did not list specialty-care hospitals such as psychiatric and rehabilitation centers. Ambulatory care, long-term institutions and pharmacies were not addressed either.

Hospitals are facing large issues such as decreasing reimbursements, over-crowding, and of course the cost of non-funded government mandates are probably contributing to most of their problems. There is that word again, "government". Government is forcing hospital emergency rooms to give "free" treatment to anyone who shows up regardless of ability to pay. They know this includes people in this country illegally and those people of our society that know they cannot be turned away and probably would not pay for services even if they could. Confront your political representative about this problem and you would probably be told he/she had nothing to do with this. The truth is he/she created a government bureaucracy that makes the rules with the power of law and there is very little recourse. Being a country boy at heart I call this "passing the buck".

Getting back to hospital trends we learn that hospitals plan on increased spending on facility replacements and expansions, and to fund new technology. There will be variations of these plans depending on access to capital. These expansion plans represent an effort to attract customers with hotel-like amenities, better customer service orientation, internet access by patients, and expanded visiting hours. Personally I think a lot of these plans are unnecessary fluff and will do nothing to contribute to healing patients.

Here are some thoughts you may not hear from any other source but they tell a story you will find interesting. One solution to our health care "crisis" we hear from our elected politicians is to spend more money, as if throwing more money at a situation will cure the problem. Looking back it is easy to compare our public school system and our health care system because both systems share something in common. Mediocrity is alive in our health care system and public schools. Our public school system is more interested in building more schools and creating more bureaucracy than in educating our children and preparing them for "life". I think it is idiotic for anyone to think that spending more of our hard earned tax dollars will fix any situation. Here is a good place to review the definition of **"idiotic"**. *"Doing the same thing over and over and expecting different results".*

Our current health care system is so convoluted there is no system to reward excellence and there is no penalty for mediocrity. It would be great if the health care system was revamped to allow free enterprise market needs to dictate the direction of health care. There are thousands of dedicated and professional people in the health care system who are not recognized properly because of government intervention. These "good" servants usually receive no financial reward for their efforts because they are guided by their moral compass and will not be a participant in questionable practices. They are excellent because of the energy and enthusiasm they put into their work. One unassailable truth about our current system is that high quality, low cost care is not financially rewarding. Just the opposite is true. Today's environment offers too many loop holes for hospitals and doctors to financially cheat if they are so inclined. It needs to be changed.

I recently read about a research study done at Dartmouth Medical School that suggested if everyone in America went to the Mayo Clinic for their health needs, our annual health care bill would be 25% lower. This calculates out to more than $500 billion annually, or about $1,667 per each and every American, AND, the average quality of care would improve. Of course, not everyone can go to the Mayo Clinic. The question is why is this example of efficient, high quality care not being duplicated all across the country? To me the answer is simple, we have a health care system created by greedy politicians and we need to take the solution out of their hands.

Here is some of what I see could happen in a normal free-enterprise market. Entrepreneurs in search of profit would solve this problem by re-packaging and re-pricing their services in order to make customers happy. Without a free-enterprise system, health care will continue with contracts and prices imposed by large impersonal bureaucracies. Doctors (physicians) will have virtually no opportunity to re-bundle their services for a different price and the result is very little entrepreneurship. Years ago professionals such as lawyers, accountants and such, discovered that the telephone was a useful instrument for communicating with clients. Try calling your doctor on the phone to discuss your health and see how rare it is to actually talk to him/her. Another technology doctors have not learned to use is "email".

THERE IS HOPE! Already in this country a spectacular type of health care service is developing and it is outside the "third party system" we have become accustomed to. This trend is "walk-in clinics" located in shopping centers and drug stores and the concept is spreading rapidly. These clinics post prices, with very little waiting, electronically maintained records, and the quality of service is comparable to traditional primary care at half the cost.

Stay with me now, you are probably wondering if this system will work for the usual hospital surgery, or is this system best suited for specialized services. Let me answer this by discussing "medical tourism" because the answer to your question is a resounding yes. If you are willing to leave this country, as many of our citizens are doing, you can have access to efficient, high quality health care. In

India, Thailand and elsewhere around the world, facilities are offering U.S. citizens virtually every kind of procedure for package prices. Packages cover all the costs of treatment, and sometimes airfare and lodging, and at prices one-fifth to one-third the cost in the U.S. Care is often delivered in high quality facilities that have electronic medical records and meet American accreditation standards.

If we look at two parts of health care, there is more reason for optimism. There is the part where *third party forces are absent* and I see a system teeming and bristling with entrepreneurship and innovation. Then there is the part where *third parties pay the bills* and I see the absence of entrepreneurship and more of the same chaos that has been the symbol of health care far too long.

You might think that health insurers and employers would find it in their self interest to break the mold. Evidence is clear that entrepreneurs raise quality and lower prices and let us remember that this principle works in every industry, not just health care. The insurance industry can make the product more attractive to potential customers. The trouble is that the entire third-party payment system is completely dominated by government, principally through Medicare and Medicaid. Private insurers tend to pay the way the government pays and providers who break Medicare rules in order to better serve the patient run the risk of being barred from the entire Medicare program. This was real life for me. As I mention in the pharmacy chapter, I owned a pharmacy when Medicare and Medicaid was thrust on us. When we complained about the idiotic system they created we were told we had to go along or the government would open their own pharmacies.

You and I need to do everything we can to prevent the kind of "socialized medicine" we see in Canada, Italy, and many other countries. Not only does socialism not work but we pay an exorbitant price for health care with our tax dollars and our time and just as important, we give up our freedom of choice.

Let's you and I not get confused with too much information. The best way to achieve our goal of a workable health care system is for us to be united in our goal. Too much information only confuses and sidetracks our effort. Patients are hungry for help so their health decisions will be easier and I will spell out a workable blueprint in this book that could bring much needed reform.

## CONCLUSION

As I see the future of health care we have two overall choices. The American people will either take responsibility for their individual/family health care, or abdicate the responsibility to the government.

Trusting the government (politicians) would be the very worst option and I hope I can convince Americans I am right. Since I am convinced that politicians are at the root of our health care crisis, let us question them about the health care plan they have chosen for themselves. After all, if it is good enough for them, they should be willing to make it available to us because they are paying for it with our tax dollars. They designed the plan to give themselves the very best, again at our expense.

The politicians will never give us the same plan they enjoy because it would bankrupt the country and they know it. While I do not know the specifics of their plan, I don't think I would be very far off the mark by saying the plan probably pays 100% of their health care needs and it costs them nothing. If you think I am off base with this opinion then think back a few years ago when it was discovered our representatives in Washington DC created their own bank and were found guilty of making loans they did not repay, wrote checks on funds that did not exist and other offenses that would be illegal in the private sector.

This wonderful health care plan for our politicians is not really what upsets me the most. The thing that upsets me the most is their pandering and condescension to the citizens of this country when it comes to health care. Their standard stump speech is about "taking care of the poor and working class and making sure everybody has health care". They are free and loose with their promises and our tax dollars, making hollow promises they cannot keep, and playing the sympathy card to buy votes. The simple truth is that it is not the government's responsibility to provide health care for everyone in this country.

For all Americans whatever we want in life, be it education, job, car, family, home, wealth, quality of life, religion and yes health care it is our individual responsibility to make things happen. We have freedom to pursue anything we want, provided it is legal, moral and will not infringe on others. Life is not easy and nothing is guaranteed. Each individual makes his or her choices and lives with the consequences.

We also have the choice and moral responsibility to take care of those less fortunate. There will always be poor citizens and I do as much for them as I can and at the same time wish I could do more. In this country the government declares "full" employment, which means that everyone is working and has a job, when unemployment is at 4.5% of our population. It is assumed that 4.5% could not, or would not work even if they could. Further, the Bible tells us that the poor will always be with us. So what do we do about health care for this segment of our society?

Even now there are churches and charitable organizations taking part in providing some of the needs of our poor and disadvantaged. Here in my home town there are food pantries, holiday chow lines, "homeless" shelters, and organizations providing counseling and limited subsistence for unwed mothers, troubled children, and the list goes on. For sure there is more to be done and I have every confidence the citizenry of this nation through benevolent organizations will rise to the occasion. All of the examples above subsist mostly on private and charitable funding as opposed to government funding.

Everything the government spends in the name of "helping the poor" they have taken from all of us in the form of taxes. Taxes that have literally been taken from us at the point of a gun and redistributed by politicians to gain votes are not what the "poor" need.

I am convinced that all of us would open our hearts and pocketbooks of our own free will, just take the gun away from the government.

So, what do we do about fixing health care in this country? It begins with declaring health care to be run as a free-enterprise, supply and demand concept. When this is accomplished this already great country will be even better and stronger. Our country will be a model to be followed throughout the world as an example of compassion, freedom, prosperity, and our overall improved health.

Let's be very, very clear about what constitutes "health care". Throughout this book I have referred to health care as two words "health care", and not one word as "health care". The dictionary I own does not list the word "health care". This means to me that there is no such thing as "health care" as a system. Health care means something different to everyone and is in fact an individual's health care needs and desires. Health care to one individual may be the desire and need to lose weight to enjoy better health. To another it may be breaking the addiction of tranquilizers or pain killing drugs, or dealing with diabetes, mental health, allergies, cancer, or any of a number of maladies.

It is very important to understand you cannot go to, or depend on, the government for good health. You cannot go to a doctor and receive good health. A doctor can help the body heal most illnesses or diseases, but just healing may not define health care. You cannot go to a hospital and find good health, but you may get relief from an illness or physical maladies. The patient may have to make some life changes to improve their quality of life. Perhaps health care is the quality of life an individual can enjoy with some effort. The problem we all have in understanding health care is that we have all been conditioned to think good health can be provided by doctors, drugs, hospitals, or political promises. We have all been duped because what we think health care to be, it is nothing more than a system of "paying" for health care needs. We can improve everything by having realistic expectations, accepting life for what it is and what we can make of it, and dealing with challenges that confront us.

The following is a guideline, or blueprint, for establishing a system for paying for health care driven by market forces.

Government's Role:

• Until such time as the IRS is abolished and replaced with a "fair tax" a big portion of individual/family health care costs should be deductible on our tax forms.

• Facilitate the movement of health care plans from state to state as our citizens move around.

• Honor current obligations to senior citizens but phase out entitlements. Allow citizens to opt out of the Social Security System if they desire and declare that below a set age Social Security is not an option.

• Make health care mistakes off limits to lawyers, or at least not very profitable for them. Mistakes happen and there are no guarantees in life. In a free enterprise system those who repeatedly may mistakes will not be successful anyway and they will have to find something else to do.

Business's Role:

• Get out of the business of providing health care for employees.

• Should be allowed to pay employees more salary to help them pay for health care needs but this would be as far as the employer's responsibilities go.

Insurance's Role:

- Design and administer basic health care plans and allow individuals/families to select the plan that best meets their needs.

- With only five or six health care plans to choose from, plans should be the same, or identical, regardless of the insurance company. This will allow people to shop for the best prices as determined by market forces without being confused by minor differences in policies. For instance: Plan A will be the same offering by all insurance companies as far as what needs are covered and deductible amounts. The cost of an individual health insurance policy, or a family policy, will vary between insurance companies.

- All plans should carry a high or catastrophic deductible.

- Tax deductible health savings account should be created that are tax advantaged and interest bearing. The funds from these accounts would be used by individuals to pay for medical services which would create an environment where some services, or operations, could be negotiated between the doctor, patient, and/or hospital. Further: If a family has a $5,000 annual deductible and they spend less because they practice and work at good health, then the unspent funds could be earmarked for retirement in a tax free environment.

- Non-essential medical needs not covered by insurance may include such things as normal pregnancies, once a year physicals, and non-life threatening illnesses. Note: Should non-life threatening events become life threatening they could be covered by insurance.

Individual's Role:

- Make sure you live a healthy life style, or a life style you can afford.
- Elect "statesmen" to public office, not politicians.

There is one element of our society that I have not talked about, but an element that can greatly affect or influence public perception and understanding of issues. This element is our news media and in no way am I suggesting curtailment of free speech. However, if the news media really cares about being a valuable part of our nation's overall moral and financial health they will have to work at presenting news that is news and not the slanted, biased opinions they currently offer us as news.

Well my friends, there you have it. A blueprint for how health care should work in this great country. My sincere hope is that everyone will seriously consider everything presented and do what you think is right. I pledge to do everything I can to promote these concepts. I am ready to make speeches, debate with anyone with differing views, even create a communication vehicle to answer questions, all to help arrive at a consensus solution that does not include government (politicians). My wife and I have children and grandchildren and we want them to have the best life can offer. If we do not fix health care, the future is not one I would want to be a part of. Health care is getting more and more expensive and benefits becoming less and less, and if not changed it will bankrupt our economy.

One last reminder, this broken health care system got started because there were enough people who desired what they thought would be FREE health care. The expectations of our citizens should be more realistic. Change will not be easy, there will be a lot of questions, some may benefit more than others during the change, but in the end, if we see this through the rewards will be worth the effort.

TO ALL, HAVE A GREAT AND BLESSED DAY!

Printed in the United States
200176BV00002B/388-576/A

9 780979 593574